T0365850

The Essential Essence

A Metaphysical view of Poetry

DR. B. G. NASH PH. D.

The Essential Essence
A METAPHYSICAL VIEW OF POETRY

Copyright © 2025 Dr. B. G. Nash Ph. D..

All rights reserved. No part of this book may be used or reproduced by any means, graphic, electronic, or mechanical, including photocopying, recording, taping or by any information storage retrieval system without the written permission of the author except in the case of brief quotations embodied in critical articles and reviews.

iUniverse books may be ordered through booksellers or by contacting:

iUniverse
1663 Liberty Drive
Bloomington, IN 47403
www.iuniverse.com
844-349-9409

Because of the dynamic nature of the Internet, any web addresses or links contained in this book may have changed since publication and may no longer be valid. The views expressed in this work are solely those of the author and do not necessarily reflect the views of the publisher, and the publisher hereby disclaims any responsibility for them.

Any people depicted in stock imagery provided by Getty Images are models, and such images are being used for illustrative purposes only. Certain stock imagery © Getty Images.

ISBN: 978-1-6632-7025-2 (sc)
ISBN: 978-1-6632-7026-9 (hc)
ISBN: 978-1-6632-7024-5 (e)

Library of Congress Control Number: 2025900519

Print information available on the last page.

iUniverse rev. date: 01/08/2025

The Essential Essence

Metaphysical Awareness

A commitment to those who have the desire

In

Becoming great leaders

Through confidence of the self

Dedication

To all the dreamers, the doers, and those who dare to defy the odds. This book is dedicated to you—the relentless souls who believe in the power of their dreams and the strength of their determination.

To those who toil in the quiet hours, turning whispers of ambition into the roars of reality, and to the ones who refuse to be confined by the expectations of others—your journey is the true testament to what it means to be successful.

May these pages serve as a reminder that success is not just measured by what you achieve, but by the courage you show in the face of challenges, the kindness you extend to others, and the passion that fuels your every step.

This book is for you, the architects of your own destiny.

Contents

Light & the Darkness

I ask, what fears have you more for, darkness? Or the lack of the light? The darkness hides our fears, suppresses tears and becomes a place of complacent.

Nevertheless, the darkness causes us to walk without sight, protecting us from awkwardness, and draws on fear for survival. This has become a safe haven for emotions hidden from the ridicule which the light might present.

Dearly I ask, how would you be able to find the very elements that brought unto you life from the womb where darkness gave birth to light? Or would you prefer to remain in the fetal only to absorb the substance created by the light. It suits you well to brave things not seen and not aware of the truth, and your only consolation is if light is so fast, why then darkness is present.

In the dance between light and darkness, we find our true selves. Embrace both the shadows and the illumination, for it is within this balance that we discover the essence of our existence. Let the light guide you, but do not fear the darkness, for it is in the unseen that we often find our greatest strength.

Tears

Tears, where are they? They used to bring peace and tranquility in times of suffering. It was the only thing I could rely on in the days of my youth without shame. It's as if a wall built with the bricks of ridicule, self-doubt and shame held together with pride. But how can this be?

I have made my way through many walls constructed by society, went through doors locked by bias and prejudice. Nevertheless, I have met my match, what tool would it take to free my tears? Should I wait until my tears overflow only to experience a rush of emotional feelings only to overwhelm?

My soul feels as if it is weighed down and my heart is waiting patiently to witness the tears that have fallen in the days of my youth. In the silence of withheld tears, we find the strength to face our deepest fears. Let the walls crumble, and let the tears flow, for it is through this release that we heal and grow.

6

Eternal, Love, Internal

Dear love, where did you leave to, you left memories of the days from my youth. You covered me with the warmth of the sun, placed in front of me people that brought happiness and joy. I long for the days past yet understanding I must grow in hoping to learn more about you. But as the days, months and years past, you have taken on many masks that are colorful, beautiful and seemly calm and pleasurable.

I took the extreme to get close to you again, only to learn that you would effortlessly walk pass my heart and toy with my mind and emotions. I beg to ask, what happened to you, why did do change? And you were kind to answer, do you love because you need? Or do you need because you love. I have always been close to you,

I watched you seeking for me searching for what you have grown to learn what love may be, and the closer love allowed you to come, you became distracted by the beautiful and colorful masks. If only you had the courage to reach for the masks, behold there love would abide. In the ever-changing dance of love, we find ourselves both lost and found. Embrace the masks and the mysteries, for it is through this journey that we truly understand the essence of love.

The Mirror in the Lake

My image I see in my shadow, my reflection I adore in my mirror, I see that it is always the same. But I am a human capable of deep thoughts, oftentimes caring and ignoring. I am curious with emotional intellect that keeps my thoughts soaring. I see myself flying, to places unknown, or is it a way of escaping the things I have outgrown.

It seems wherever I imagine myself, I see the same in the mirror, a one-dimension person with an abundance of error. Oh, to myself I say, imagine flight take me to the lake where my image is taken from the mirror to a place where life itself reflects my deepest thoughts. I see my image moving with every ebb and flow, I see my image as calm, becoming more beautiful as if it is lending me, it's wisdom of endurance, proving to me that I to can become stable even though I flow.

I will no longer wonder which reflection of myself matters, but I will share the wisdom which says "which person shall matter the most, the one in the mirror? Or the one flowing in the lake. In the stillness of the mirror and the movement of the lake, we find the true essence of ourselves. Embrace both reflections, for it is through this duality that we understand our own depth and beauty.

Oh mind, speak to your heart

Oh mind, speak to me, we share the same place where life began for us, yet you ignore me. You have held for ransom beautiful things that may make me feel confident and loved, you have witnessed and handed me trauma and the pleasure of recovery you have kept to yourself.

Oh mind, your choices, your decisions, reflect selfishness which I feel the guilt and shame only to suffer with feelings of loneliness. But we are never apart because when you need air, I will send it to you, when you need the energy for your thoughts, I will always supply and yet to you pass me by as if I only matter when the hurt and guilt is handed down, only separated by the commands you give a voice to,

Oh mind, even though we are not on the same page, we are in the same body till death do us part. In the silent dialogue between mind and heart, we find the essence of our being. Embrace the tension and the harmony, for it is through this interplay that we truly understand ourselves.

Survive to Live

I survive to preserve my physical needs; my soul survives to reach a higher plane. I would choose the physical to let my soul find the way, hoping to hitch a ride when the higher plane is met. But how would the physical self-learn to accept such a change. I long to reintroduce myself as one and not divide myself among the entanglement of survival.

When do we live, when is it known to us the difference, when will we learn to become one once again, our inheritance to live. Living after survival is a gentle transition, for the sake of all self-willed persons, learning how to survive may be the goal of the physical, but the soul yearns to become one with what the soul is attached, and while the physical reaches out and around, the soul reaches up and outwards.

I beg of you, look up, then begin to look outwards. In the delicate dance between survival and living, we find our true purpose. Embrace the journey, for it is through this balance that we discover the harmony of our physical and spiritual selves.

Potential, why hide thyself

We all have been told stories of our possibilities, what may happen when thoughts, our dreams are planted in "endless possibilities". What would it take to make these possibilities come true? Should we depend on others to point the way? Or just trust in what society deems possible? External possibilities are dependent on and deeply implanted in the environment of choices, influence and self-respect.

Would realizing this make our dreams, hopes and aspirations come true? Become a tangible fact? So many questions have come to possibilities it confuses me so, as one question would take a stand, where do possibilities rise from? Look inwards, I am the spark which causes the fire of all possibilities. I am not energized until all possibilities have played their part in your journey. I become alive to share with your new beginnings.

I am potential, unrealized ability and my strength is patience and hope. When you rest and hold fast unto faith, I will reveal the potential rendering you new possibilities. In the quiet moments of reflection, we find the spark of potential within us. Embrace the journey, for it is through patience and hope that we unlock the endless possibilities that lie ahead. Honestly and truly yours, potential.

The Journey of Loss and Discovery

Life is full of lost and found stories. We express what is found for what it is, what is lost may well become complicated to accept. I lost something I held very dear to me. I became clouded with anger; foggy thoughts would prove consistent with layers of confusion seasoned with loneliness. I was not concerned with asking why but wanting to know how to find the warmth of the sun.

I lost something, what or where do I find? Then I began to realize, here I still stand. Patience became my salvation, devastation offered mercy and loneliness blended into the light. You may ask, what did I find? Could it be the essence of self? Or could it be explained and simply, although we experience lost, it is the story told that lives on forever in a very special place.

In the end, what I found was not just a resolution to my loss, but a deeper understanding of myself. Through patience and acceptance, I discovered that every story of loss is also a story of growth and transformation. And though we may lose what we hold dear, the essence of our experiences lives on forever in a special place within us.

18

Precious or Sacred

What is deemed precious, held close to us, what secrecy does it require? We all hold something or a fine jewel handed down through the ages. Precious is crafted of both substances, linked emotionally, deeply feeling a special closeness. Nevertheless, does precious deserve rules? Boundaries drawing a fine line in the sand?

After all, it is special in so much that we hide precious things, place them in a place where only we can access in privacy. Because when precious is exposed, others would place on it a value with offerings of equal worthiness to prove fair trade. Now, let us give thought to a presence, what if we give in to a tempted enquiry, aware of the precious relationship joining through memory and experiences.

What then would we feel if what we hold sacred was valued? In the end, what we hold precious and sacred is not just its material value, but the emotional and spiritual connection we have with it. These treasures, whether tangible or intangible, are best kept close to our hearts, protected from the world's scrutiny. For in their true essence, they are priceless and irreplaceable, woven into the fabric of our being, and shared only with those who truly understand and cherish their worth.

Success or Failure

Success, you stand tall, as a bonfire of light, A testimony to dreams, to campaigns fought right. You bring joy, a sense of delight, A moment where all doubts subside. But Failure, you linger, as a shadow in the night, A reminder of lessons, of struggles in sight. You bring growth, a chance to learn, A fire within, a passion to burn.

In the dance of life, you both play a part. Success and failure, intertwined from the start. One cannot exist without the other, For in each, the seeds of the other we discover. Success, you are the summit, the peak we seek, Failure, you are the valley, the path unique. Together, you weave the fabric of fate, A journey of growth, a story great.

Embrace them both, with open heart, For they are not worlds apart. They guide us forward, hand in hand, Through life's vast and wondrous land. In the end, success and failure are not mere outcomes, but integral parts of our journey. They shape our experiences, mold our character, and guide us towards growth and understanding. Embrace them both, for they are the twin pillars that support the edifice of our lives, leading us through the highs and lows and teaching us the true essence of resilience and perseverance.

22

A Balance of Temperament

Oh temperament, you shape my days, with a dance of moods, in countless ways. You guide my thoughts, my actions too, a silent but loud force, both old and new. In instants of calm, you bring me peace, a gentle breeze, a sweet release. But when the storm within me brews, you stir the depths, ignite the fuse. You are the balance I strive to learn, to steady my hand, resisting me through.

The anchor in life's shifting sand, resembling the tempest wild, a force untamed, a restless child. Oh temperament, are you the key to understanding the depths of me? For in your ebb and flow, I find the essence of my heart and mind. Through highs and lows, you lead the way, a guiding light, both day and night. In your embrace, I learn to balance, the true reflection of my very being. In the end, temperament is not just a fleeting mood, but the essence of our inner world.

It guides us through the calm and the storm, teaching us to find balance and harmony. Embrace your temperament, for it is the key to understanding the depths of your being, and in its ebb and flow, you will discover the true reflection of your heart and mind.

Uncertainty, Sufficient or Necessary

In the remnants of our minds, uncertainty finds a home of necessity. A whispering presence, at first thought seems sufficient. We follow our dreams in a safe place, with hopes uncertainty remain elusive and what is sufficient prevails. Yet what we seek remains out of reach, but reachable. We learn how to find what is both sufficient and necessary. Through the fog of doubt, we wander, searching for answers, a place to belong.

Our hearts yearn for clarity, a guiding light, to lead us through the uncertainty, to find resolution. But perhaps it's the journey, the journey for truth, that shapes our desires from our earliest days, when fear of uncertainty was no longer necessary. It is for the delicate balance of what is sufficient and what is necessary, we discover strength and grace. Embracing the reachable, we find our place.

So let us not fear the uncertain path we tread, for it's in the seeking that our souls are nourished. What we truly need may not at first seem sufficient, but in the pursuit, we find it necessary to respect our fears. In the end, uncertainty is not just an obstacle, but a vital part of our journey. It challenges us to seek clarity and understanding, to balance what is sufficient with what is necessary. Embrace the uncertainty, for it is in the pursuit that we find strength, grace, and our true place. Respect your fears, for they guide you towards what is truly necessary in life.

26

Whispers of the Metaphysical Self

In the quiet depths of the soul's embrace, imposing the variety of the physical. Its domain is earthly, giving the laws of nature dominance. But there lies a realm, a beauty not seen, existing beyond time and space, where neither physical nor conscious rule. A whispering echo has made its home, subconsciously a place of rest and restless contemplation, a silent call, the metaphysical self, transcending all. The restlessness of my subconscious thoughts, stemming beyond the veil of flesh and physical foundations, where thoughts and dreams are freely sown into conscious potential. The embroidery of light and shadow weaves, in the heart of existence, where the spirit breathes. Infinite journeys through the mind's conscious awareness, where questions linger and answers avoid reality. I long for a dance with the essence, pure and free, unbound by the chains of reality. In the stillness of the inner sea, the metaphysical self yearns to be A beacon of truth, a guiding spark, illuminating the path to who we are. Embrace the mystery, the unseen thread, that weaves through life, where angels tread. For in the depths of the soul's own light, the metaphysical self takes flight. In the end, the metaphysical self is not just a fleeting thought, but the essence of our true being. It transcends the physical and conscious realms, guiding us towards a deeper understanding of ourselves. Embrace the whispers of the metaphysical self, for they illuminate the path to our inner truth, weaving through the fabric of existence, and allowing our spirit to take flight.

Greetings,

I hope you enjoyed my work. I made every effort to convey the importance of both spiritually and naturally looking internally for the answers we all seek. In the following pages, I emphasize the meaning of each poem, hoping to further entice your curiosity towards the person you aspire to become. In some way, these pages provide a third perspective, allowing the reader not only to be left with a poem and its reflective picture but also an explanation of the work. I have entitled this section "Quiet Introspections," with the hope that it will add more meaning and depth to your experience. Throughout my professional and personal life, I have dedicated myself to helping others who ask, "Why do I have to go through all this?" and "Is this really necessary?" These are complex questions that cannot be fully answered in this context. However, they deserve all the attention and consideration we can give.

Gratefully Yours,

Dr. B. G. Nash, Ph. D.

Quiet Introspections for each poem

Light & the Darkness

"Light & the Darkness" delves into profound themes and presents a thought-provoking perspective. The image explores the duality of light and darkness, questioning which is more fearsome and examining the roles they play in our lives. This is a powerful theme that resonates with many readers. strong metaphors, such as "the womb where darkness gave birth to light," which adds depth to your exploration of these concepts. The imagery of darkness as a "safe haven for emotions" and light as a potential source of ridicule is compelling. he poem exhibits a philosophical tone, prompting readers to reflect on their own fears and perceptions of light and darkness. This introspective quality makes the poem engaging and thought-provoking. language is evocative and poetic, with phrases like "suppressing tears" and "brave things not seen." The poetry structure allows your ideas to flow naturally, enhancing the contemplative nature of the poem. The use of questions throughout the poem invites readers to engage with the content and reflect on their own experiences and beliefs. This interactive element adds to the poem's impact.

Overall, "Light & the Darkness" is a beautifully crafted and intellectually stimulating piece.

"Tears"

The poem captures a profound sense of longing and introspection deeply moving and introspective. The imagery of tears as a source of peace and tranquility in youth is powerful and relatable. The metaphor of a wall built with "bricks of ridicule, self-doubt, and shame" is striking. It effectively conveys the emotional barriers that have been constructed over time. The imagery of doors locked by bias and prejudice adds to the sense of struggle and perseverance. Language is evocative and poignant. Phrases like "weighed down" and "waiting patiently to witness the tears" convey a deep sense of yearning and emotional weight.

The tone is reflective and contemplative, inviting readers to empathize with their experience. The poetry verse allows thoughts and emotions to flow naturally, enhancing the introspective quality of the poem. The use of questions adds a sense of searching and uncertainty, which is fitting for the theme. The theme of emotional suppression and the longing for release is powerful. The poem explores the complexities of emotions and the impact of societal expectations on personal expression.

Tears" is a beautifully written and emotionally resonant piece.

Eternal, Love, Internal

Eternal, Love, Internal" is a poignant exploration of love and its complexities. The poem delves into the evolving nature of love, reflecting on how it changes over time and how our understanding of it deepens. This theme is relatable and thought-provoking. vivid imagery, such as "masks that are colorful, beautiful and seemingly calm and pleasurable," to convey the different facets of love. The metaphor of love wearing masks adds depth to the poem, illustrating how love can be both alluring and elusive. Language is evocative and introspective.

Phrases like "you left memories of the days from my youth" and "toy with my mind and emotions" convey a sense of longing and introspection. The tone is reflective and contemplative, inviting readers to ponder their own experiences with love. The poetry allows thoughts and emotions to flow naturally, enhancing the introspective quality of the poem. The use of questions adds a sense of searching and curiosity, which is fitting for the theme. The poem effectively communicates a deep connection with love, portraying it as a constant presence that evolves and changes. The dialogue with love adds a personal touch, making the poem feel intimate and heartfelt.

"Eternal, Love, Internal" is a beautifully written and emotionally resonant piece.

"The Mirror in the Lake"

This is a beautifully introspective piece that explores self-reflection and personal growth. The imagery of the mirror and the lake is powerful. The mirror represents a static, one-dimensional view of oneself, while the lake symbolizes a dynamic, evolving reflection. This contrast effectively conveys the theme of personal growth and self-discovery. language is evocative and poetic. Phrases like "deep thoughts, oftentimes caring and ignoring" and "wisdom of endurance" add depth to the poem. The tone is reflective and contemplative, inviting readers to ponder their own self-perception and growth.

The poetry allows thoughts and emotions to flow naturally, enhancing the introspective quality of the poem. The use of questions and internal dialogue adds a sense of searching and self-exploration. The theme of self-reflection and the journey towards self-acceptance is relatable and thought-provoking. The poem encourages readers to look beyond the surface and embrace their evolving selves. The poem effectively communicates a deep connection with oneself, portraying the journey of self-discovery as a continuous process. The imagery of the lake's ebb and flow adds a sense of movement and growth.

"Oh mind, speak to your heart"

This is a powerful exploration of the relationship between the mind and the heart. The poem delves into the internal conflict between the mind and the heart, highlighting the struggle for balance and understanding. This theme is deeply relatable and thought-provoking. vivid imagery and metaphors to convey the tension between the mind and the heart. Phrases like "held for ransom beautiful things" and "separated by the commands you give a voice to" effectively illustrate the emotional struggle. language is evocative and poignant.

The tone is reflective and contemplative, inviting readers to ponder their own internal conflicts. Phrases like "feelings of loneliness" and "till death do us part" add depth to the poem. The poetry allows your thoughts and emotions to flow naturally, enhancing the introspective quality of the poem. The use of direct address to the mind adds a personal and intimate touch. The poem effectively communicates the interconnectedness of the mind and the heart, portraying them as two parts of a whole that must coexist despite their differences. This adds a sense of unity and complexity to the poem.

"Survive to Live"

This is a profound exploration of the relationship between physical survival and spiritual growth. The poem delves into the duality of physical and spiritual existence, questioning how we can reconcile the two and achieve a higher state of being. This theme is deeply philosophical and thought-provoking. strong metaphors, such as "the physical reaches out and around, the soul reaches up and outwards," to illustrate the different directions of physical and spiritual pursuits. The imagery of looking up and outwards adds a sense of aspiration and transcendence. language is evocative and contemplative.

Phrases like "entanglement of survival" and "gentle transition" convey a sense of struggle and hope. The tone is reflective and introspective, inviting readers to ponder their own journey towards unity and higher understanding. The poetry allows your thoughts and emotions to flow naturally, enhancing the introspective quality of the poem. The use of questions adds a sense of searching and curiosity, which is fitting for the theme. The poem effectively communicates the longing for unity between the physical and spiritual selves, portraying this journey as a continuous process of growth and self-discovery. "Survive to Live" is a beautifully written and intellectually stimulating piece.

"Potential, why hide thyself"

This is a thought-provoking exploration of the concept of potential and the journey to realizing it. The poem delves into the nature of potential and the factors that influence its realization. This theme is deeply philosophical and encourages readers to reflect on their own potential and the steps needed to achieve it. strong metaphors, such as "I am the spark which causes the fire of all possibilities," to illustrate the idea of potential as a latent force waiting to be ignited. The imagery of potential as a spark and fire adds a sense of energy and dynamism to the poem. language is evocative and contemplative.

Phrases like "endless possibilities" and "unrealized ability" convey a sense of hope and aspiration. The tone is reflective and introspective, inviting readers to ponder their own journey towards realizing their potential. The poetry allows your thoughts and emotions to flow naturally, enhancing the introspective quality of the poem. The use of questions adds a sense of searching and curiosity, which is fitting for the theme. The personification of potential as a character that speaks directly to the reader adds a unique and engaging element to the poem. This approach makes the concept of potential feel more tangible and relatable. beautifully written and intellectually stimulating piece.

"I lost something, I found something"

The poem explores the emotional journey of losing something dear and finding solace and understanding in the process. This theme is deeply relatable and resonates with many readers. vivid imagery, such as "clouded with anger" and "foggy thoughts," to convey the emotional turmoil of loss. The metaphor of "loneliness blended into the light" adds a sense of transformation and hope. language is evocative and contemplative. Phrases like "patience became my salvation" and "devastation offered mercy" convey a sense of growth and resilience. The tone is reflective and introspective, inviting readers to ponder their own experiences with loss and discovery.

The poetry allows your thoughts and emotions to flow naturally, enhancing the introspective quality of the poem. The use of questions adds a sense of searching and curiosity, which is fitting for the theme. The poem effectively communicates the journey from loss to self-discovery, portraying it as a continuous process of growth and understanding. The idea that "the story told lives on forever in a very special place" adds a sense of enduring hope and meaning.

"Precious or Sacred"

This is a profound exploration of the concepts of value and intimacy. The poem delves into the distinction between what is precious and what is sacred, questioning how we value and protect these aspects of our lives. This theme is deeply philosophical and encourages readers to reflect on their own values and boundaries. vivid imagery, such as "a fine jewel handed down through the ages" and "drawing a fine line in the sand," to illustrate the delicate nature of what we hold dear. The metaphor of precious things being hidden and sacred things being held close adds depth to the poem. language is evocative and contemplative. Phrases like "linked emotionally" and "shared sparingly amongst those who understand" convey a sense of intimacy and reverence.

The tone is reflective and introspective, inviting readers to ponder their own experiences with what they hold precious and sacred. The poetry allows your thoughts and emotions to flow naturally, enhancing the introspective quality of the poem. The use of questions adds a sense of searching and curiosity, which is fitting for the theme. The poem effectively communicates the importance of recognizing and respecting the value of what we hold precious and sacred. It encourages readers to consider the boundaries and protections they place around these aspects of their lives. a beautifully written and intellectually stimulating piece.

"Success or Failure"

Beautifully captures the intertwined nature of these two concepts. The poem explores the duality of success and failure, emphasizing that both are essential parts of the journey of life. This theme is deeply relatable and resonates with many readers. vivid imagery, such as "bonfire of light" and "shadow in the night," to illustrate the contrasting nature of success and failure. The metaphors of success as a summit and failure as a valley add depth to the poem, highlighting the highs and lows of life's journey. language is evocative and poetic. Phrases like "testimony to dreams" and "a fire within, a passion to burn" convey a sense of aspiration and resilience. The tone is reflective and encouraging, inviting readers to embrace both success and failure as part of their growth.

The poem's structure, with its balanced stanzas and rhythmic flow, enhances the contemplative quality of the piece. The use of parallelism, such as "Success, you are the summit, the peak we seek" and "Failure, you are the valley, the path unique," adds a sense of harmony and balance. The poem effectively communicates the idea that success and failure are not opposites but rather complementary forces that guide us forward. This message is empowering and encourages readers to view both experiences as valuable. a beautifully written and inspiring piece.

"A balance of Temperament"

This is a beautifully introspective piece that explores the complexities of temperament and its impact on our lives. The poem delves into the dual nature of temperament, highlighting its role in shaping our thoughts, actions, and emotions. This theme is deeply relatable and encourages readers to reflect on their own experiences with temperament. vivid imagery, such as "a gentle breeze, a sweet release" and "the tempest wild, a force untamed," to illustrate the contrasting aspects of temperament. The metaphors of calm and storm effectively convey the ebb and flow of emotions. language is evocative and poetic. Phrases like "a silent but loud force" and "the anchor in life's shifting sand" add depth to the poem.

The tone is reflective and contemplative, inviting readers to ponder their own journey towards balance. The poem's structure, with its rhythmic flow and balanced stanzas, enhances the contemplative quality of the piece. The use of questions adds a sense of searching and curiosity, which is fitting for the theme. The poem effectively communicates the idea that understanding and balancing our temperament is key to self-discovery and personal growth. This message is empowering and encourages readers to embrace their emotions and strive for balance. a beautifully written and emotionally resonant piece.

Uncertainty, Sufficient or Necessary

The poem continues to explore the balance between sufficiency and necessity within the context of uncertainty. The addition of respecting our fears adds a new layer of depth, emphasizing the importance of acknowledging and understanding our emotions. The structure remains clear and the flow is smooth. The transitions between lines and stanzas are well-maintained, making it easy to follow the progression of thoughts. Language is evocative and thought-provoking. The imagery remains vivid, with phrases like "remnants of our minds," "fog of doubt," and "delicate balance" enhancing the reader's engagement. The new lines about respecting our fears add a powerful and relatable element.

It continues to resonate on an emotional level, addressing common human fears and desires. The new emphasis on respecting our fears adds a sense of compassion and self-awareness, making the poem even more impactful. It remains unique with its exploration of uncertainty and the interplay between sufficiency and necessity. The new changes offer fresh insights and perspectives that are both relatable and profound. It is a compelling and thoughtful piece that effectively captures the essence of uncertainty and the human quest for understanding. The new additions enhance its depth and emotional resonance.

Whispers of the Metaphysical Self

The poem uses rich and evocative language to create vivid imagery. Phrases like "the embroidery of light and shadow" and "a beacon of truth, a guiding spark" add depth and beauty to the poem. effectively explores the theme of the metaphysical self, delving into the distinctions between the physical, conscious, and metaphysical realms. This provides clarity and depth to the reader's understanding.

evokes a sense of wonder and introspection, inviting readers to reflect on their own metaphysical selves. The lines about the restlessness of subconscious thoughts and the longing for a dance with the essence add emotional depth. maintains a consistent structure and rhythmic flow, making it easy to read and follow. The transitions between different realms of existence are smooth and coherent. "Whispers of the Metaphysical Self" beautifully captures the essence of the metaphysical journey with enhanced imagery, clarity, and emotional resonance.

A Self Enquiry

I am very intrigued about how the human mind responds to the essences that exist all around us. In my personal experiences I find myself responding differently to the essences, than just a reaction to external distractions. Humans respond differently to essences and external factors due to a combination of psychological, neurological, and environmental influences.

Essences and Internal Perception:

Essences refer to the intrinsic qualities or core aspects of something, often tied to personal beliefs, values, and emotions. These are deeply internal and subjective.

Our response to essences is shaped by our individual experiences, memories, and emotional states. For example, a poem or a piece of music might evoke strong emotions because it resonates with our personal experiences and inner world.

External factors are stimuli from the outside world, such as sights, sounds, and physical sensations. These are processed through our sensory systems.

Our response to external factors is often more immediate and can be influenced by our current environment and physical state. For instance, a loud noise might startle us, or a beautiful landscape might bring us peace.

Different parts of the brain are involved in processing essences and external factors. The limbic system, which includes the amygdala and hippocampus, plays a crucial role in emotional responses and memory, influencing how we perceive essences.

Sensory information from external factors is processed by the sensory cortices and then integrated with other brain regions to form a coherent perception of the environment.

Our psychological makeup, including personality traits and mental health, affects how we respond to both essences and external factors. For example, someone with a high level of empathy might be more deeply moved by a poem.

Cultural background and societal norms also play a role. Diverse cultures may place varying levels of importance on internal essences versus external appearances.

Philosophically, existentialism posits that our essence is not predefined but is shaped by our choices and actions. This perspective emphasizes the importance of personal experience and the subjective reality of each individual.

In summary, the interplay between our internal world and external environment, along with our unique neurological and psychological makeup, leads to varied responses to essences and external factors. This complexity is what makes human experience so rich and diverse.

Philosophical & Scientific Anatomy

In the labyrinth of neurons, thoughts entwine, A symphony of synapses, electric and divine. Gray matter whispers secrets of the mind, In folds and creases, consciousness we find.

The cortex, a canvas of dreams and fears, Paints our perceptions, through the years. Hemispheres in dialogue, left and right, Logic and creativity, day and night.

Deep within, the hippocampus guards, Memories of laughter, love, and scars. The amygdala, sentinel of emotion's gate, Guides our passions, love, and hate.

Cerebellum, maestro of movement's grace, Coordinates our steps, our dance, our pace. Thalamus, the relay of sensory streams, Filters reality, shapes our dreams.

In this intricate organ, mysteries reside, The essence of self, where we confide. A universe within, vast and profound, In the brain's anatomy, life's meaning is found. I thought adding this to my collection may provide an appropriate approach to what comes next.

The frontal cortex

In the realm of thought, the frontal cortex reigns, A conductor of reason, where intellect gains. Executive decisions, crafted with care, In this cerebral palace, wisdom lays bare.

It plans our futures, maps out our goals, Guides our actions, and tempers our souls. Impulse and judgment, balanced with grace, In the frontal cortex, we find our place.

Creativity blooms in its intricate folds, Imagination's playground, where stories are told. Personality's core, our essence defined, In this brain's frontier, our true selves we find.

Emotion and logic, a delicate dance, In the frontal cortex, they both have a chance. A guardian of ethics, of right and wrong, In its neural pathways, our morals belong.

So, here's to the cortex, frontal and wise, A beacon of thought beneath our skies. In its depths, humanity's light does shine, A testament to the wonders of the mind.

In the quiet chambers of the mind, Where neurons spark and thoughts unwind, A poem whispers, soft and clear, Awakening senses, drawing near.

The frontal cortex, sharp and bright, Analyzes each word, each line's light. Patterns and rhythms, it seeks to find, In the dance of language, intertwined.

The limbic system, deep and true, Feels the emotions, old and new. Joy and sorrow, love and fear, In poetry's embrace, they all appear. The hippocampus, memory's gate, Stores the verses, small and great. Echoes of stanzas, long and brief, In the brain's archive, they find relief.

The amygdala, with passion's flame, Ignites the heart, calls out by name. A poem's power, raw and grand, In the brain's response, we understand.

Synapses fire, connections made, In the realm of poetry, thoughts cascade. A symphony of mind and heart, In every poem, a work of art. In the web of life, the nervous system weaves, A network of signals, where the body perceives. From the brain's command to the spinal cords embrace, Nerves transmit messages, with elegant grace.

Sensory pathways, alert and keen, Detect the world, both seen and unseen. Touch, taste, sound, and sight, In the nervous system, they all unite.

Motor neurons, swift and precise, Guide our movements, with no need for advice. From a gentle touch to a powerful stride, The nervous system, our trusted guide.

Autonomic rhythms, steady and true, Regulate heartbeat, breath, and more too. Sympathetic sparks, in moments of stress, Parasympathetic calm, in times of rest.

In this intricate dance, balance is found, A symphony of signals, profound. The nervous system, a marvel to behold, In its depths, life's mysteries unfold.

I believe in the power of poetry; it speaks softly yet firmly to the soul of those seeking profound answers to the simplicity of life's ebb and flow. It takes a good person to stand for the good of others and in the face of adversity become steadfast.

Dr. B. G. Nash, Ph. D.

The concept of essential essence transcends the physical and delves into the very core of existence. It is the intrinsic nature that defines the true identity of an entity, beyond its external attributes and transient states. This essence is immutable, a timeless truth that remains constant amidst the flux of the material world. It is the purest form of being the fundamental quality that gives rise to all manifestations and experiences. To grasp the essential essence is to perceive the underlying reality that connects all things, a profound understanding that transcends the superficial and touches the very heart of existence.

In the realm of psychology, the concept of essential essence pertains to the core attributes that define an individual's identity and personality. It encompasses the fundamental traits, values, and beliefs that remain consistent over time, shaping one's behavior, thoughts, and emotions. This essence is the bedrock of self-concept, influencing how individuals perceive themselves and interact with the world around them. Understanding one's essential essence can lead to greater self-awareness and personal growth, as it allows individuals to align their actions with their true nature, fostering a sense of authenticity and fulfillment.

Thank you so much, may the love you seek always remain known.

Dr. Bruce G. Nash, Ph. D.

Printed in the United States
by Baker & Taylor Publisher Services